The TRUTH ABOUT ELVES

by Thomas Kingsley Troupe   illustrated by Robert Squier

PICTURE WINDOW BOOKS
a capstone imprint

Thanks to our advisers for their expertise, research, and advice:

Elizabeth Tucker, PhD, Professor of English
Binghamton University, Binghamton, New York

Terry Flaherty, PhD, Professor of English
Minnesota State University, Mankato

Editor: Shelly Lyons
Designer: Lori Bye
Art Director: Nathan Gassman
Production Specialist: Jane Klenk
The illustrations in this book were created digitally.

Picture Window Books
151 Good Counsel Drive
P.O. Box 669
Mankato, MN 56002-0669
877-845-8392
www.capstonepub.com

Printed in the United States of America in North Mankato, Minnesota.
032010
005740CGF10

All books published by Picture Window Books
are manufactured with paper containing at least
10 percent post-consumer waste.

Library of Congress Cataloging-in-Publication Data
Troupe, Thomas Kingsley.
  The truth about elves / by Thomas Kingsley Troupe ; illustrated
by Robert Squier.
    p. cm.— (Fairy-tale superstars)
  Includes index.
  ISBN 978-1-4048-6047-6 (library binding)
  1. Elves—Juvenile literature. I. Squier, Robert, ill. II. Title.
  GR549.T76 2011
  398.21—dc22
                        2010000900

Watch for Elves!

Elves are magical creatures that live in forests and caves, and near springs. But are they real? Some people believe so. Others think elves are make-believe characters in stories.

History of Elves

Elves first showed up in Scandinavian stories. No one is sure how elves came to be. Today, there are many different elf stories.

Elves are sometimes called "hidden folk." They are often confused with dwarves, gnomes, or fairies. All of these creatures look like small people.

In some stories, elves live a long time. They can be 100 to 1,000 years old. In other tales, elves live forever and do not age.

Elves come in all shapes and sizes. Some elves are as tall as people. Others are small enough to hide in a flower.

pointy ear

bright, almond-shaped eye

pointy chin

What Do Elves Look Like?

Most elves are said to be beautiful. They have long, skinny bodies and perfect skin. Their bones are light, so they can run quickly.

Most elves have pointy ears and chins. Their almond-shaped eyes are bright. Many elves dress in beautiful clothes.

perfect skin

beautiful clothing

skinny body

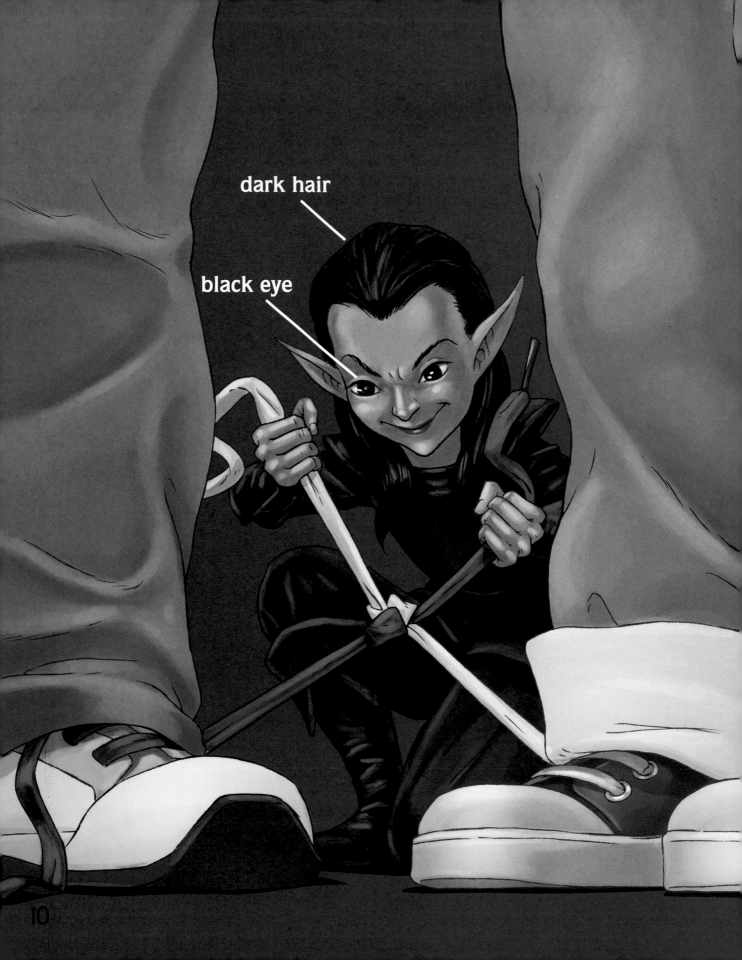

dark hair

black eye

But dark elves look different than most elves. Dark elves have black eyes and hair.

Where Do Elves Live?

Most elves choose pretty places to live, such as areas near springs, waterfalls, or mountains. If you find a peaceful area, there might be elves nearby!

Legends say most elves like to stay hidden. They will move their homes and families if people come near. Elves will also fight to protect their homes.

Because elves love the outdoors, some live inside trees. Others sleep in fields of flowers.

Some elves prefer to live in mounds of earth. They have secret doors that lead in and out of their hidden homes. Dark elves live underground and in the shadows.

15

The North Pole is different than other elf homes. In this cold, snowy place, elves build toys every Christmas season. Santa Claus would have to close his workshop if it weren't for his elves.

Magic Dust

Elf Behavior

Elves don't help others often. But good elves do use magic to help kind, hard-working people.

Elves trick people into looking away while they perform their magic. That way they can hide their magical secrets.

Elves are said to gather in meadows on misty mornings. They form circles, then dance and sing. Legends say if people watch, bad things may happen.

Some elves are troublemakers. They like to play tricks on people. A dark elf might whisper bad dreams into someone's ear.

Elf Stories

In stories, elves have special skills. Sometimes they do things in secret. Other times people watch the elves performing.

The Elves and the Shoemaker is about an old man who makes shoes. Each morning he wakes up to find beautiful shoes that have already been made.

One night, the shoemaker hides and watches. Small elves sneak into his shop. They make the shoes for him. To say thank you, the shoemaker sews tiny clothes and shoes for the elves.

In *The Elf Mound*, the elf king wants the goblin king to marry one of his seven daughters. The daughters show their special dancing and magic skills at a feast. The seventh daughter's skill is storytelling. The goblin king chooses her to be his wife.

Elves Everywhere

Today elves appear in books, movies, and even TV commercials.

Author J.R.R. Tolkien included elves in his *The Lord of the Rings* series. He enjoyed the creatures so much, he made up languages for them.

A star shines on the hour of our meeting.

Elves Today

Elves are still popular in today's world. People love them as much as they did when they first appeared in fairy tales.

Friendly or mean, helpful or shy, elves still delight us. But are they real? Well, what do you believe?

Legend Has It

- If a person watches elves dance, time moves quickly. Years pass as if they were only hours.

- Sometimes dark elves appear hollow if seen from behind.

- Some elves are thought to be invisible. That makes them even harder to find!

- People used to stay away from areas where they believed elves lived. They didn't want to disturb the elves.

- Though light and dark elves are most common, other types of elves include sea elves, mountain elves, and sky elves.

Glossary

goblin—a mischievous, dwarflike creature from stories

hollow—having a hole or empty space inside

legend—a story that seems to be true and is handed down from earlier times

meadow—a grassy area

mound—a hill or pile

Scandinavia—the area of land that includes the countries of Norway, Sweden, and Denmark; many also consider Finland, Iceland, and the Faroe Islands part of Scandinavia

spring—a place where water rises up from underground and becomes a stream

Index

To Learn More

More Books to Read

Cech, John, retold by. *The Elves and the Shoemaker*.
    New York: Sterling Pub., 2007.

Dorman, Brandon. *Santa's Stowaway*. New York: Greenwillow
    Books, 2009.

Knudsen, Shannon. *Fairies and Elves*. Fantasy Chronicles.
    Minneapolis: Lerner Publications, 2010.

Internet Sites

FactHound offers a safe, fun way to find Internet
sites related to this book. All of the sites on
FactHound have been researched by our staff.

Here's all you do:

Visit *www.facthound.com*

Type in this code: 9781404860476

Look for all the books in the Fairy-Tale Superstars series:

The Truth About Dragons

The Truth About Princesses

The Truth About Elves

The Truth About Trolls

The Truth About Fairies

The Truth About Unicorns